PIGLETS

Sandie Lee Books

Piglets

There are around 2 billion pigs found on the planet and they all started out as piglets (baby pigs). Pigs are used by humans for food and for other products. Some pigs and their piglets are even kept as pets. Even though we may say someone is "pigging out," pigs actually eat quite slowly and enjoy the taste of their food. In this article we are going to discover more fascinating facts about piglets, like what they eat, how they grow and so much more.

Where in the World?

Did you know piglets and their parents are found all over the world? Piglets live with their mom on farms. Here they are usually kept in a barn. The piglets will be housed with their mother in what is known as a sty. These small compartments keep the piglets safe and warm.

The Body of a Piglet

Did you know piglets look the same as babies as they do as adults? Piglets are born being stocky with shorter legs and a curly tail. They can weigh from 2 to 4 pounds. Depending on the breed, the piglets can vary in color. The piglet is also covered in short soft bristles.

The Piglet's Feet

Did you know the feet of a pig and piglet are called trotters? These animals have 4 toes on each foot. These are pointed downwards and end in hooves. The hooves are very tough and protect the piglet when it is running or walking. When the piglet walks it uses the tips of its toes, rather than its whole foot.

A Piglet's Nose

Did you know the snout of a piglet is highly tuned? The nose of the piglet is round and flat, with large nostrils. The nose of a pig is also very flexible with lots of muscles. As the piglet grows, its nose will become tougher. This will allow the piglet to sniff and root around in the ground.

What a Piglet Eats

Did you know piglets drink milk from their mother? Newborn piglets will nurse milk from their mother. After about 4 weeks the piglets will start to sample solid food. As they grow, piglets will eat a diet of corn, wheat, oats, barley and other grains. Piglets will also root around in the ground to find insects and worms.

The Piglet's Special Ability

Did you know piglets are highly social? Piglets like to be close to each other. They are also very smart and clean. Piglets grow into pigs that will continue close bonds with one another and can even grow close to other farm animals. Most piglets and pigs are gentle animals unless threatened.

The Piglets as Prey

Did you know wild piglets have predators? Wild boar piglets can be hunted by large predatory animals such as large cats, bears, wolves and humans. Domesticated farm piglets are less likely to fall victim, but can still be hunted by wolves, coyotes and predatory birds. Most piglets are kept safe inside of a barn or pen.

Piglet Talk

Did you know piglets can make lots of different sounds? Piglets will squeal very loudly when they feel scared or threatened. As they grow, they will be able to make around 20 different sounds. Piglets learn at a very young age to recognize their mother's voice. A mom pig will even "sing" quietly to her babies.

Piglet With Mom

Did you know a mother pig can have up to 12 babies in one litter? Mom pig is pregnant for 4 months before she gives birth. She is very protective of her babies and will even fight to keep them safe. Mom pig feeds all her baby pigs at one time. She does this by lying on her side.

Piglet Play

Did you know piglets like to play? Just like a dog, piglets like to run, chase and play. They will play with buckets, feed sacks, cardboard boxes and most anything. However, they do tend to get bored of the same toy very quickly. Piglets also squeal and make noise when they are having fun.

Sleeping Piglets

Did you know piglets like to sleep all together? Piglets like to sleep in a large group, all snuggled against each other. Their favorite position is nose to nose with another piglet. It is also thought that piglets and adult pigs dream, very much the same way we humans do.

The Growing Piglet

Did you know piglets are fully grown at 3 years old? Male piglets grow to be called boars and female piglets will be called sows. Male piglets will grow large tusks when they are adults. These are actually its two front teeth. Piglets grow up quite quickly and can live to be around 15 years-old.

The Wild Boar

The wild boar piglet starts out its life in a nest of moss, leaves and other nesting material. It is well hidden in a thick forest or bush. There can be anywhere from 4 to 6 wild boar piglets in a nest. This species of piglet has light brown fur with cream and brown colored stripes down its back.

The Vietnamese Potbelly

This species of piglet can make a great pet. This pig originated in Vietnam and was later domesticated as a pet. It tends to stay smaller as an adult pig, is clean and very smart. It is black in color and has tough, bristled hair. It also has a big round belly.

Quiz

Question 1: How many pigs are estimated to be in the world today?

Answer 1: Around 2 billion

Question 2: How big is a piglet at birth?

Answer 2: Anywhere from 2 to 4 pounds

Question 3: What are the feet of a piglet called?

Answer 3: "Trotters"

Question 4: What special thing does a mother pig do for her babies?

Answer 4: She "sings" to them

Question 5: What is the favorite position for a piglet to sleep in?

Answer 5: It likes to sleep nose-to-nose with another piglet

Thank you for checking out another addition from Sandie Lee Books! Make sure to check out Amazon.com for many other great titles.

www.ingramcontent.com/pod-product-compliance
Lightning Source LLC
Chambersburg PA
CBHW050802290526
45792CB00008B/2295